Pine Cones & Rhubarb
& Little Hissy Kisses

Jocelyn Munro

Pine Cones & Rhubarb
& Little Hissy Kisses

Thanks

To members of NEW Inc, past and present: it has been an ongoing delight to be part of the group these many years. I deeply appreciate my association with you. To writing and other friends in New Zealand, thank you for the long conversations, adventures in the hills and mountains of home and far away places, and for the ginger wine with 'flash ice creams' on frosty Friday nights. You know who you are.

A brief note about Francesca: internet friends for many years, both of us writers and artists, we connected at a deeper level. Her passing several years ago still leaves a sense of sadness. In memory of our friendship, one of the poems is hers. It was originally included in one of my Art Zines.

How can I fully express my heartfelt gratitude to Stephen and Brenda Matthews for their friendship, encouragement and extreme patience? This must be the longest-in-the-making publication of the decade. Thank you. I cannot bow low enough before you.

Finally to my family, Clare and Greg, and Nathan and Linn: I am so grateful for your ongoing love and support. To my six grandchildren, Tyler, Finn, Anton and Rose in New Zealand, and William and Olivia in Adelaide, you are the stars in my night sky. You fill my life with blessings and I love you all dearly.

Pine Cones & Rhubarb and Little Hissy Kisses
ISBN 978 1 76041 666 9
Copyright © Jocelyn Munro 2019

First published 2019 by
Ginninderra Press
PO Box 3461 Port Adelaide 5015 Australia
www.ginninderrapress.com.au

Contents

Pine Cones & Rhubarb	7
Little Hissy Kisses	8
Aftermath in New Orleans	9
Christmas Day	11
Bullet Points	12
Rainbow	13
Unquiet Night	14
Fool	15
Circus	17
Clock	18
Wild Night	19
Night Trek in Fjordland	20
this man	21
Tabula Rasa	22
The Sweetest Life	23
Sunday Market Musings	24
Sunday Markets 2	25
Storm and Peace: an Installation	26
Subversion	27
Spaghetti Petals	28
South Canterbury Bus Ride	29
Sounds of Love	30
Sitting in the sun on King William Street	32
Shadow Dance	34
Plains Birds	35
Remember Mary?	37
Terrible Beauty	38
Mary (found poem)	39
Languishing: a Practice	40
Knight Ride	41

Kingfisher	42
Just one poem	43
Indigo Inkstrokes	44
Hot Peppery Eggs	45
Under the sea on top of the world	46
Helambhu – Langtang	47
Melamchi Gaon	49
Evening Breeze	50
DJ60: Over the Tasman	51
Disturbed	52
Dawn Service: Anzac Day	53
Cooling Earth	55
Code For Girls	56
Breadcrumb Carpet	57
Alighted	58
At the Rugby 7s, 2008	59
At the Zine Fair, 2008	63
At the Zine Fair 2	65
Central Market	67
First & Many	68
Note to Francesca	69
South Canterbury Landscape: views from the bus	71
Still Life: Cut Glass Bowl With Pebbles	72
This vessel of a woman	73
Moonbird Dream	74
Times	76
White Boats	78
Winds	79
Air	80

Pine Cones & Rhubarb

you brought me gifts
of pine cones & rhubarb
tenderness   and wood for the fire

you came to me with kindness
joy wine &   gin
and you folded my clothes before you left
after drowning me in exquisite kisses
& the sweetest loving

you brought me the gift
of your warm skin   soft against mine
of laughter   fun
deep conversations & chit chat
you held my eyes in yours and shook me
with your gifts of passion and desire

you brought me gifts which all too soon
were gone   gone
but still   i wished to bring to you
the gift of thanks   such heartfelt thanks
for all the gifts you brought to me

Little Hissy Kisses

the sea licks the
edges of the
sand with its
little hissy
kisses and I
stroll along   the
sun hot against
my back

Aftermath in New Orleans

i am black   see
i sit here in the ruins
of this place
i called my home
and all   all   is devastation

my white sister sat beside me
at first
at first   before the bulldozers
came in to clear the
devastation away   but
she got up and left to go
and supervise them
at her place

i haven't seen her since

they tell us that people
are moving back here
i think it's true

they told us we'd get
help to rebuild our homes
our lives
i think it's not true

now, tonight, in a home in
a far-off land
a white woman watches
and despairs for me
when she sees a white
man on the television, and hears
him say
i don't want them back
keep them out

i am black see

This poem was written after listening to a black woman on TV in New Orleans. It was about three months after the 29 August 2005 hurricane Katrina, and many, if not most, of the black residents had still not had much assistance.

Christmas Day

Mum's belly is huge
Mum   are you expecting
don't talk like that   it's not nice

are you?

never you mind   that's no way to talk

Mum's washing fruit for salad
Grandma's putting freshly podded peas in a pot
Aunty Esther's whipping cream
all in Grandma's tiny scullery

they're preparing Christmas dinner for 14
11 days later my first brother is born

Bullet Points

i need a critical incident report he said
bullet points only   a page will do

what's with bullet points anyway
who called them that
bullet connotes attack   aggression   hit first   kill   defeat
victory

why not heart points
heart points connote differently
greater opportunity
for peaceful resolution
guns laid on the ground
all parties still standing

i won't argue with that   he said

bullet-free points   favourably received

Rainbow: A Garden in Fairbanks, Alaska

violets open shy faces to the sun
indigo vibrates in their shadows
merging with the blue of Himalayan poppies
standing to attention amidst several shades of green
yellow and orange marigolds sparkle at the sun
hot red petunias gather tightly in a pot near the open door
the garden a mnemonic of virgins in bed giving you odd reactions

Unquiet Night

tonight there is scant rest for the weary
let alone the wicked
wind rattles windows
scrapes eucalypt branches against the roof
carries sounds of dogs barking

restless nights when eyes are wide shut
open unseeing
closed full of images
wide awake

when   just as you're falling asleep
thunder crashes
two cars roar up the hill
cats fight under your window

wide awake and eyes shut
on an unquiet night

Fool

fool she is
sits atop a chimney cloud
camouflage for hidden meanings

fool-hearted   she sees clearly
across the stars
to pretending hearts
disguised in foolish fashion's finest
cover for anguished souls

fool she is
breaking all the rules
entertaining naysayers
speaking truths which no one believes
soaring on her chimney cloud
running races with the moon

fool she is
making men frown
the sun smile
peering from her fluffy perch
switching brains to upside down
concealed   in foolish frippery
as she jigs a tap dance on
her chimney cap

fool she is
storyteller
stands on her head and says
sleep on it
upright she takes calculated risks
then cartwheels to the moon
speaks with the innocence of children
steps off the cliff to begin her journey
courageous   and bold

fool she is
being herself
she garners sideways glances
wraps them in sandpaper
and hangs them on trees
pretending   she nods silently
at watching faces
gathers all the raw edges around her
weaves them   boils them
and sews a fine bag
to hold pretend thoughts
with clarity   innocence
and wisdom

fool she is

This was inspired by spectacular chimney-shaped clouds I observed as we flew towards rough weather on a Sydney–Melbourne flight. Some were developing mushroom-like caps. It was a short hop, step, and a jump to imagine a figure on top.

Circus

a tisket   a tasket   a red and yellow basket
all aglitter   bangles & spangles
i wrote a letter to my love about
frozen moments in a dream playground
then put it in my pocket

i wrote tranquil and discerning predictions
full of sacred promises of leaping jumping rage and provocation
gave myself wings to tango over the rainbow
jitterbug while flying kites and doing a samba
through tears   rain and mist

in sleeping and waking dreams
i dropped it

i wrote a letter to my love
in rain and mist i dropped it

Clock

'that clock
the voice of our lives
secret thread of our weeks'
ticked away the hours
of love

the regular beat
the constancy
the monotony
finally the indifference
the harsh ticking
the rhythm
the constancy
on & on
until love was gone

first three lines from Pablo Neruda's 'Ode to broken things'

Wild Night

in the middle of the wild night
dogs bark   roosters crow
a bucket scuds a quickstep
this way and that
while magpies chatter nervously in their sleep
clutching their perches   toes tightly curled

darkness fades in a secret hush
a swooping bird rides a current
down the gully

silence settles on the morning

Night Trek in Fjordland

walking the moonlit track
stepping in and out of snow-soft
knee-high footprints
the come-again   go-again breeze a knife edge
dusting a shiver over me
bright snow across high tops above
gleams cold and eerie

this man

i see this man as he walks away from me
he is here and not here
embedded in my soul and
the cells of my body

he leaves me;
and each day anew
he leaves me again,
and i too grow cold from
his absence

all our yesterdays are sometimes
barely enough
to warm me again when
i see and feel him near to me;
untouchable now,
but so alive in my soul

what is time but moments strung together?
now and now and now and now.
there is no end to it, only change.

what was real is becoming other-real
as touchable and untouchable merge
into the everyday

i see this man moving from
shadow to light;
in me forever
for time beyond time

I wrote this poem for Eadie Abernethy when her husband Steve, a cousin of my father, died. It is what came to me as I was trying to begin a condolence letter to Eadie.

Tabula Rasa

today i wake   my heart
turned towards the sun
bright spear-beams of light momentarily
blotting out memories of all my befores

am i beginning this day with
a strong heart
what if it's true

The Sweetest Life

mine is the sweetest life
and yet
it could be sweeter still

there are things i do
not have   pretend
i do not miss though
sometimes know that missing
is missing

i need to make it
a mission to come upon the missing pieces
with great intention

Sunday Market Musings

mushrooms! $2 a box! $2 a box!
a whole box!

beautiful white coffee-froth caps
lunch and dinner for two days
mushrooms on toast
mushrooms and chicken
it's a done deal

strawberries!
three for five! three for five!

Sunday Markets 2

people bake under fierce sun
seek out the shade of stallholder tents
reject dry looking carrots for fresh juicy ones
pick out 10 plump gorgeous ripe tomatoes
listen to conversations in many accents and languages
pick their way along narrow isles
avoiding tent poles   shopping trolleys   treading on toes

watermelons look too good to be true
as if someone had painted them onto their skins

picture perfect.

Storm and Peace: an Installation

upturned lifeboats upstage the setting sun
fluoro-orange hulls crowned
by dazzling light on their bright beams

chaos erupted
volunteer coast watchers rescued boat after boat
from the unpredicted storm passing through hours ago
not one life lost

floating candles lie along the foamy edge of the water
a reminder of the hour before the storm
when boats and candles floated on calm waters

flotilla for peace

Subversion

i am astonished to learn
that the ancestors of today's silkworm,
of the order Lepidoptera,
(spinners of that most precious thread),
have been domestically raised for some
five thousand years;
the road to complete dependence on
the engineering of its human codependent.
a small winged creature,
raised like hens and ducks, cattle and sheep,
unable now even to fly;
carrying instead its useless wings aloft
as it lives its few-days-long life
subverted wholly to the profit industry

imagine that

the idea of this
unwittingly surrendered freedom
provokes a certain dismay
at my own complicity

Spaghetti Petals

my gaze raises as
gum flowers burst spaghetti petals
from cream crowns on green heads

wind disperses the crowns to the ground
in rich cream spaghetti snow

the eucalypt stretches tall
myriad crowns
stir majestically in the wind

South Canterbury Bus Ride

heading home for Christmas 2004, South Island, New Zealand

the bus heads south through St Andrews
where you can put your left arm out
of the window and tickle the sea
with your little finger
and at a stretch
with your right arm
you can cup the tops of the mountains
with your hand

land rolls
and curls
between mountains and sea

Sounds of Love

i hear you in the silences between
desultory conversations
the paper-thin sound of turning pages
and the crackle and soft whump
of logs settling on the fire

your sound is the sound
of pouring tea filling cups
spoons stirring sugar
the brief rattle of the spoon on the sink bench
and the clink of the cups' precise
placement on glass coasters

you were in the moan of the wind over high-topped mountains
in the hand steadying me across fast-flowing streams
(a different hand climbing a cloud covered pass above
Melamchi Gaong)
and in the low fresh sounds of leaves brushing over
backpacks and jacket sleeves

you are discernible in the sharp crack of
an axe splitting wood
the thud of the wood stack growing
in hens clucking round feet by the wheat barrel
and the hiss of an iron pressing linen

it's in the bursting laughter of jokes
songs in the shower
the knife-beat of chopping onions
and plates being warmed
in the microwave

you are there in the broom-swish on steps
the fumble of a key finding the lock
at the top of Mapoutahi Pa watching moonplay on the quiet sea
in the crinkly sound of hair
tickling the back of my neck

it's there in the paper-thin resonance of
hands gliding over skin
in the alert reading between the lines
and the stillness of eyes meeting
it's the hushed ba-bump of a heartbeat in the night

Sitting in the sun on King William Street

on her way from NZ
to Scotland
Diana sits in the Adelaide sun
elbow on table
hand crooked with two fingers pointing as
if making rabbit shadows

it is cardigan cool, the low
winter sun casting long shadows
across the street behind her

were it summer, it could be
eight of an evening, and not a
cardigan in sight

Diana the wise woman
adventurer traveller
philosopher fool

she's nobody's fool
do not try to fool her
she'll know even before
the thought has formed
in your head

elegant eclectic
white-haired
she is vibrant in words and gestures
vibrant with spots stripes
and   designer label

coffee cups
long empty and cold
sitting in the sun
with Diana

Shadow Dance

twilight   music skirls among the trees
the beat of a slow dance
leaves shivering
sun colour bleeding into last light
far away to the west

skirl and beat sing to me
i move with a shadow dancer
to the music

my heart remembers other places
other dancers

the music stops
as last light slides over the horizon

Plains Birds

there is so much sky here
a great upturned bowl of blue
disorientating me   used
as i am
to hills and mountains which
keep me grounded on the land

the upturned bowl is a
worry-free flight path
for small bright green parrots
jetting a path over tall
blue-green eucalypts

in this space i am lost
vertigo grips me
there's no land in sight
to hold on to
to keep me from floating away

sulphur-crested cockatoos screech
and wheel in tight formations
looking for foes
letting them know who's boss out there

the land falls away   unseen   to the west
dry   parched   thirsty land
forced to give its very life to
line the pockets of immigrants
hungry for wealth of another kind

crows 'cr a a ah k' their philosophy
sitting in the eucalypts
they harvest only what they need
and leave the rest

my hand rests on a fence post
dry grass around its base an elegant frill
the lavender-purple of a jacaranda
sings its colour to the sun

mina bird players
make the tree a theatre for
their noisy productions

plains birds high flyers
noise makers
colourful streakers
over the flat land

Remember Mary?

remember Mary?
you know Mary with the little lamb
that lamb never did have fleece as white as snow
not here anyway because soon after
it was born it was the
colour of red/brown dust

see the lambs   the bus driver said
where? i said   not seeing anything
that fitted the lamb idea
in my head

over there   he said   and suddenly
i could see brown lambs
lambs not knowing that
it's only a geographical accident of birth
which camouflages
what they might have been elsewhere

does a snake know   i wonder
that dust-brown lamb is tender in the eating
or is it fooled   spending endless
weeks in the sun   looking for the colour of snow

Terrible Beauty

like a lost memory
thoughts of winter winds
grumbling and sighing
on their passage through tall eucalyptus
awakens a cool shiver over my heat-soaked body

the canyon breathes its fiery heat
its waters giggling and gossiping
over shallow not-quite rapids
urgent on its way to a sea
it can no longer find

in the desert above the rim, eagles soar
stretching wings on wind-sighs
studying the far-below for fragile
sun-kissed prey
itself not obscured from an eagle's laser-sharp vision

diamond peak grimaces at its drying foot   at
the fast-flowing river's waters   continually diverted
manipulated   until   shrivelled and shrunken
they pound their glorious fury over
and round tumbled rocky falls
a living parody of the once-was

Mary (found poem)

there's something about Mary
she shares her home with monkeys
serves them rolls on iceberg lettuce
with mint leaves

they moved in when they found her
outside the deli
best move they ever made
it was an unexpected twist in her life

i built a prototype shed   she said
to watch a solar eclipse
the monkeys opened the sky lids
they want to unlock the secrets
of the pyramids in Mexico

in the event the eclipse was a blip
on a cloudy horizon
the pyramids reveal only
glimpses of local flower sellers
telling stories of facelifts & magical tunnels
in a perfect world   the earth-friendly monkeys
make difficult decisions   to suit the style of their Mary

there's something about her

Languishing: a Practice

languishing
is the best i can do
in these temperatures

five days of 40C knocks the breath out of me
by morning tea – lunchtime on a good day

languishing is the fine art of survival
breathe   drink water   breathe   languish

have it down to a fine art,
it's not elegant   not pretty

Knight Ride

it occurs to me
after riding through the night on the Knight Rider bus
from Dunedin to Christchurch
that i have not now had any sleep
for some 26 hours
and i can barely keep my eyes open
while i wait for a plane here at Melbourne airport

i find my eyes wide shut more every now
than then
they're tripping up my thinking brain
and i feel like an old car
coughing and spluttering myself into life
on a cold morning

a boarding call urges me
to stay awake for five more minutes

my ears are telling my eyes all about it

Kingfisher

you fly
tilting a clear
blue flash across my
sight. before you
wheel…and
unfold
orange

Just one poem

task: write just one poem
before I hang out the washing
on another hot Adelaide day

one poem   about towels on the line
a sheet   2 pillowcases   underwear
(who's counting)
a shirt   the dog's collar
what can i say
you've heard it all before

Indigo Inkstrokes

indigo inkstrokes brush lowering cloud
pushing the sunset into the sea
bright red-orange and pale yellow-orange
frame the palest green layer
like sandwich fillings stacked
at the edge of the darkening land

i watch as the horizon-light slips smooth as skin on skin
away from colour   away from light   into soft   dark   night
bright-light colours flare one last hurrah
sinking…sinking…

ladies and gentlemen   time please

Hot Peppery Eggs

Catie loves hot peppery eggs
I love hot peppery honey
I like egg yolks   firm   not hard
Catie likes her's runny

Under the sea on top of the world

in the mountains near Tangboche
i walked on fine white sand,
hot as it would be on any beach in summer.
sand and shells at twelve thousand feet
and i breathing the
thinning air of the Himalaya.

in another age i would have been
using my gills to breathe under water
in that exact place.

that was when i was Persephone,
and Demeter roamed the mountains.

Helambhu – Langtang

Sermanthung

we have nothing to which
to compare the taste of
butter tea

have nothing to which
to compare the ritual making
of butter tea
in a long tube with a plunger

nothing to which
to compare in our homeland
this immaculate clean-floor
dining
sitting cross-legged on thick warm
yak-wool mats   our hostess
plunges and plunges the yak butter
in the tube of tea

to what would I compare
my delight?

Tarkeghyang

sitting in sunshine
air mildly warm yet crisp
on white plastic picnic suite
this tiny village
2,600 metres above sea level with neither
road nor runway access
inspires a long remembered longing
for the peace and beauty
of this place   these people
and the rigours and simplicity
of less-though-amply-sufficient.
watching half a dozen village men
hand-sawing and planing twenty-foot timbers
running up three-floors-high bamboo ladders in bare feet
two sometime three
long timbers balanced over
their shoulders

medieval building methods before my eyes
take me back to the 50s
in my father's shed.

Melamchi Gaon

one foot after the other
bowed body struggling in
cold   thin   cloud-filled air

slowly slowly
up up
one foot after the other
one foot after the other

five hours climbing   through forest
beautiful moss-covered rocks
soft moss-floored ground
and dead branches dripping crystal drops
from wet mosses and lichens
in the thin cold air

slowly   slowly
climbing
over 1,500 thousand metres up up
from Melamchi Gaon
to the pass high above
slowly   slowly   madame   slowly   slowly

Pherwa reaches behind
takes my hand
and for a few moments
our breath seems
shared and easy

one foot after the other
one foot after the other

Evening Breeze

wind stirs the palms
leaves rustle
like paper skirts
wind stirs
paper skirts rustle
palm leaves

wind

DJ60: Over the Tasman

what if we were flying upside down
would i figure that the tiny whitecap birds were waves
the blood rush to my head
or the sound of the engines change as
its myriad beats rolled off into the ether

would i stick my apple in my eye in an act of dislocation
and voices float to the roof-floor of the cabin before
gravity called them back

would the stars be fireflies on the dark sky-earth ground
or the moon be our landing place
the seat belt strain against the weight of my thighs
or the exterior surfaces of drinking straws be
conduits for waterfalls of tea and whisky

what if we were flying upside down

Disturbed

my return is heavily perfumed
by the smell of you on my skin
you are in my hair
disturbing senses used to equilibrium

days later the smell of you
brushes past my senses still
where does it come from
you are nowhere to be seen
or heard

the memory of you
palpitates
and shimmies a zigzag
through me
unsettling

reminding me
that my completeness
is not quite

Dawn Service: Anzac Day

Of a sudden, standing on North Terrace on this dawning day
I hear the sound of guns booming both far away
and nearby all at once.
They are too close for comfort.
Lest we forget.

The road beneath my feet turns into the muddy bottom
of this hellhole trench where I stand,
quiet, rooted to the spot, gun ready;
waiting for the tumult and shouting to die down.
The crowd is silent amidst all the carnage that surrounds me,
listening to Anzac tributes, birds, and the first plane of the day
passing overhead on its way in to land.
In the morning, we will remember them.

The quiet is the unreal: screams and shouts
punctuate the frenzy of sound in my head,
guns and bodies are exploding around me, and
the noise blocks my vision, though I shoot, at anything,
or nothing, I do not know.
Amid the encircling gloom, oh lead, Kindly Light.
Please lead.

The crowd around me unaware, believe
they are in another time and place,
sombre, comfortable, safe.
They hear only a brass band:
Abide With Me. Lead Kindly Light

Oh, God, abide in me!
Abide in me as this hell breaks loose all around me.
Oh, God! I scream as the mate beside me is suddenly
raining over me, his blood and body parts,
his eye rolling off the top of my hand.
Age shall not weary him. Can I ever forget?

I am cold, and wet, mud glues my boots to the
bottom of the trench;
I cannot see. There is blood in my eyes.
I can taste it, it is in my mouth.
I smell it through the pores of my skin. My mate is dead.
Oh, God! Oh, God! Where are you leading me?!
God of our fathers, where are the captains and the kings now?

Now, it is quiet once more.
I am in a crowd listening, remembering
the mate whose blood gave me
today,   today,   all my todays.
I have remembered him.

Save for a choir singing hymns of salvation and commemoration,
all, all is quiet.
The Lord is my Shepherd. I shall not want.

Cooling Earth

through the glass veil   afternoon shade cools the day
too early for summer
the glimpse of a few sun dappled leaves
remnant of the day's brightness

cold seeps into the house
cold draughts skirt corners
outside it's bending trees

a few gold leaves hold the sun on the ground
as if shielding the cooling earth in a rotting carpet
waiting for frost
were it time   i would pull the blankets around my ears

Code For Girls

look what happened to pink
the subtle shades have been subsumed
to artificial lolly colours
bright and as in your face
as a temple monkey stealing your earring

the turning away from the girl colour
has been reversed in the name of
marketing and profits
the insidious turning of the wheel
awful   devious   clever
sickening

how easily little girls and their mothers are seduced
to become the seducers

no mind of their own is sufficient to resist

Breadcrumb Carpet

on a lawn amongst lush patches of verdant green
the drought dry grass crunches under my feet
as if it were a breadcrumb carpet
making audible footsteps which would otherwise be unheard
or at most only the soft-pad sound which disturbs
neither ants   nor mice   nor men.
trees shed leaves
branches
bark
unable to slay the thirst of this
the hottest summer in 100+ years
unable to hold themselves together
until the cooling of autumn

in this mad heat i must lick their trunks
make them better

earth has turned to shades of ochre powder
dusting my toes with summer warmth
leaving my feet as those of an unkempt waif

in all the barefoot summers of my growing
i have no recollection of such never-ending
daily earth-powdering
until in this   my 60th   year

Alighted

sitting   listening
suddenly feeling
the soft warmth
of your cheek
against mine

dark eyes
hold mine for
this brief eternity

lightning zigzags
through the centre
of me

At the Rugby 7s, 2008

this is my annual opportunity to give voice to my Grand Canyon river call
woooowoowoowoowoowoo!

I can be heard in the crowd yet few will hear me   woohoo!

i cheer the Kenyons (underdogs against the French) loudly
wooooowoowoo!
as two young men in nun's habits walk by   pious
beers in hands   raising their glasses   blessing passers-by

again i cheer the long legged   desert running Kenyons
while at the same time memory shifts & once again we are
slipping into the tongue of Lava Falls Rapid
trepidatious   tense   exhilarated   wooooowoowoo!
underdogs almost always deserve a river call

between every game music booms like waves
crashing in a force 4 storm   silencing me

everything changes quickly   as fortune smiles
back and forth in the chaos
chaos is necessary to give birth to these dancing stars

it's time to cheer loudly for the Cook Islanders playing the Kiwis
i cheer for them because they're the underdogs
and because the Kiwis are well ahead   woohoo?

three   of five   young men dressed
in fluorescent aerobic gear and wigs
are doing a slinky wiggle in front of a camera
later i learn that they   too   are Kiwis   Go the Kiwis!

four hours later I am once more cheering the Cook Islanders
playing against Argentina   Go! Go! GO!
in this place the feral in me slips out to play
at half-time the score is even   woohoo!

strutting by in their gorgeous finery are four pirates' women
topped with marabou-trimmed tricorn hats
they will surely seduce every pirate worth his salt
who happens by   woo-hoo-hooo!

four young Aborigine lads saunter past   nonchalant
though first people in this land and oldest known people anywhere
here at the Adelaide Oval they are the minutest minority
that's how it is   few people will wonder about it

Japan   newcomers in the rugby world
are valiantly catching up on Wales   old hands
each goal and try a very woowoo moment

Fred Flinstone and Barney amble by
going back the way they came

at 6.30 on this balmy autumn evening
the sun dips its farewell at the eastern stands
while game #20   Canada versus the USA   plays itself out
Canada the favourites now ahead
as the cooling air turns slightly shivery
overhead lights out-do the sinking sun
bare skins goosebump
and the US score last minute to win   woohooo!

the music has quietened to force 2
perhaps in accord with the darkening day
a lull during interval gives me time to remember other cool evenings
in the faraway canyon
soft sand a carpet underfoot
gourmet dinners from the camp kitchen
a welcome repast at the end of the day

all of a sudden   music booms at force 4 again   while a drumbeat
a violin   and a tin whistle echo from the canyon
every now is then also

Kenya the underdogs are playing Fiji
strong contenders to win the competition
the man in front of me is advising them how best to play
sounding as if he is shouting inside a tin can
he is too far away to be heard

perhaps they did hear him   by osmosis   through their cells
they play his moves then score

for a little while i want Kenya to win
i also want Fiji to win   they are part of
who I am   from the South Pacific

in the end the winning doesn't matter too much
the game well played is what matters

the sky deepens to indigo
cathedral spires glow in their left of centre stage lights
an All Black hop-skips off the field amidst genteel applause
whilst a team-mate scores another try   running rings
around the Scottish opposition who have no score at half-time
when Scotland scores twice i cheer extra loudly
New Zealand is my home   my blood is Scottish
a wee bit of me wants them both to win

sixteen nations played today   Titan dominating Titan
David playing Goliath   Samoa beating Fiji,
South Africa dominating the game with Australia
and the final against New Zealand

somewhere a chirruping mimics the twilight sound of
the tiny butterfly bats at Lees Ferry in the Canyon
i call a last time as the final teams walk off the field
wooooowoowoowoowoowoo!
and the raft slides once again down the tongue of a rapid.

At the Zine Fair, 2008

At the Zine Fair in
Balfours old factory in
Elizabeth Street, Adelaide,
I saw a man in leopard skin tights
with a hot pink belt slung low around his hips,
open shirt above showing off his bare torso
as he played his air guitar and accompanied himself with madrigals,
at times raucous and loud.

He accompanied also the singer, (on his left),
herself a loud and interesting purveyor of the art.
She had something red tied around her dark hair.
Boots on her feet.

To her left, I saw a man in tattered jeans, the crotch tattered
beyond what most would call 'decency', but seeming to me an
ingenious device for cooling,
on this 15th day of the heat wave.

Would that I could be so brave.

He played his air guitar and sang his madrigals as if he were,
himself, also the fourth and fifth members of the band.
He played and sang with gusto,
at times raucous and loud.

Would that I could be so brave.

At the end of each song
the crowd cheered and clapped and whistled.
The accolades well-deserved.
I sighed with relief that I could enjoy the performance,
no longer needing, as once was the case, to judge them all
'more than a bit beyond the pale'.

At the Zine Fair 2

At the Zine Fair, I saw a young woman,
slender and beautiful, in high-waisted leggings,
midriff a little bare and
cropped top tied at the front, with lacy bra
exposed,
beautifully.

She had black Doc Martin-style boots on,
rich dark maroon velvety-looking gloves,
and a crimson velvet hat,
all to protect her from the 40-degree heat.
She was so beautiful.

I saw a young man, with hair that stood up in perfect
imitation of an electric shock.
I do not know what he was wearing.
I liked his face.

I saw a young woman in pale shorts,
and singlet top with spaghetti straps,
just-got-out-of-bed hair,
and bluish-pink long thick socks.
She did not seem to notice the sizzling 42-degree heat.

I saw a woman in black, grey, and white striped trousers and
black T-shirt, her brown hair well-cut.
With her her young teenage son and daughter
nice kids, good manners, nicely dressed, fashionable-ish,
brown hair like their mother's.
She was interested in the Artist Trading Cards
and bought the small zine, with a view to having a go. She is
a scrapbooker.

The young teens also pored over
the copies of original cards,
wanting to touch them in spite of
the flat plain of the paper,
the tactile quality of the originals apparent
and mysterious
all at once.

I saw a man, greying hair close-cropped,
frequently staring at who knows what,
frequently surrounded by fans
of his zines, his philosophies, his collegiality.
I saw him in animated conversations.
I did not see him smile.

I saw zinesters lying on bright coloured bean bags
in front of fans stirring the air;
conversations were desultory, quiet, heat-soaked.
I saw a man, sound asleep it seemed.
I had heard him talking of heat and exhaustion;
he was working there, would finish late into the night.

As in a mirror, I saw a woman, softly greying
light sandy-brown hair pinned high,
curls tumbling archly round her face.
I saw her animated, I saw her quiet,
I saw her watching.

Central Market

Friday night at the market
people come and go
slow slow quick quick slow

heads down   heads up
scurrying   parading   ambling   striding   hobbling

slow slow quick quick slow
people come and go
yellow pants with crocs to go
soft shoulder bags   and hippy skirts
tailored suits   black leather shoes
woollen cardigans   houndstooth skirts

couples   singles   threes and fives
laughing   listening   drifting away
animated   indifferent   living lies
filling in the time and void
before going home
some of them alone

people come   people go
slow slow quick quick slow

looking at watches
looking around
breathing in the colours
staring at the ground
slow slow quick quick slow
people come and go

First & Many

i am first daughter
grandchild   niece   grand-niece   cousin-to-be

i became friend
girlfriend   wife   mother
aunt
next came student   teacher   role model   lover
artist   poet   writer

now I am mother-in-law   grandmother   grand-aunt

                c
           r   o   n
                e

          wise one

a glistening star with many points

Note to Francesca

dear Francesca
hello!
here i am   at last

thank you so much
for sending me
your titbits and news
while i have been 'off air'.

actually
i feel a bit like I'm coming up
for air after many
particularly busy weeks

it's hard to believe you're already talking about fall
are you sure
i didn't think
it was that long ago
that you were mentioning
late snow on the ground

downunder   spring is
shaking her blossoming head at the breeze
showering the ground with pink and white petals
as if she were at a wedding.

officially, it's still winter here
not yet time to put thermal clothes away
we've had practice runs for spring,
a warm day here and there
interspersing the cold and wet

The air I come up for is
spring's own palette to keep
me on my toes as
I dance
to her variable rhythms.

the inchoate promise of
that palette
keeps me on tenterhooks waiting for more

warmest regards

jco

South Canterbury Landscape: views from the bus

riverside / roadside / seaside
mountainside
cowside / cloudside / shedside
sheepside
thistles and bracken
buttercups and creeks

Still Life: Cut Glass Bowl With Pebbles

cut glass glitters;
pebbles shine an invitation
to hold their smoothness
in the warm palm of my hand

oily rainbow colours;
soul-deep blue
dense silver
peppermint white
clear limpid green

pebble gleanings

This vessel of a woman

Ripe as molten glass
gathered at the tip
of a glassblower's pipe –

plain words,
clear words, her words
pour forth

to a man whose
presence
prompts her wetness

to an unfamiliar old
woman
crossing a crowded street

to a child on the edge
of self-sufficiency.

After the solitude and
silence
of gathering herself,
this vessel of a woman
speaks,
'Let me, now, take your
hand'

Frances Norton Honich

Moonbird Dream

i dreamed a moonbird walked into my room
        the night black
swirling leaves tangling
its feathers
        shadows and mist tangling
        its footfalls and
darkness tangling it breathless

i dreamed it called to me, a
husky whisper
        where is there light?

there is no light i said
only darkness I said
the swirling and tangling carrying my voice
gentle as a butterfly wing
disturbs the air into a faraway storm

i dreamed it called to me
        soft and unsure
there is light
        its sound close to me
        swirling, disturbing the air

& i dreamed the mist
and the swirling and tangling
were suddenly still

in a faraway voice rising
deep from within me,
as soft as a butterfly rests on a rose,
i reminded the moonbird
she is the light and even
in darkness
she just has to shine

Times

there were times when i thought i can't do this
i can't take one more step in all this snow
as we creep at snail's pace
to the top of the high mountain pass
i can't climb the steep side of the canyon in the searing heat
i can't make my way along this narrow ledge
70 feet above the canyon floor below

i can't keep going to reach Ghandruk with Delhi belly
i can't leave this man I've loved for so long because he can't commit
i can't leave town on my own & make a new life elsewhere

there were truths i couldn't face because i was afraid of what
i would have to do with them
there were lies i told because of the fear
there was water i could not sail on because it was over my head
a yacht i would not sail in because i might tip out

there was a mother i could not face often enough
because of the pain of her anger and bitterness
a niece i could not help because i did not know where to begin

still i took one more step in the snow
eased my way along that narrow ledge
climbed the steep side of the canyon
though the air burnt my lungs and sucked the energy out of me
reached Ghandruk even with Delhi belly
left the man I'd loved so long
made a new life in another city
faced truths even when i didn't know what to do with them
sailed in water over my head
in wild wild weather i never tipped out

now i remember my mother with
compassion and gratitude
support family in small ways
remember the relief of doing more with less
and the fruition and completion

learnt that there is nothing to fear

White Boats

dinghies beached on heavy grey metal
like bleached whalebones
empty dinghies minus oars
clean as porcelain cups empty of fluids

how long have they been there
so clean   yet they look as if they have been there
for a very long time

thoughts quicken around what happened
the sometime presence of strong women
had they wept silently, heart mourning
the watery deaths of children and lovers

the scene is full of questions

Winds

when the winds of Grace blow
i stand
at the top of the hill
waiting
while the uninterrupted flow
whispers secrets
on its way by

when the winds of Grace blow
my hands catch the secrets
whirling on the breeze

holding them softly
my heart listens
intently

Air

i am air sign
libra of the scales
i am the air in which the scales float
and move
in the delicate dance of justice
and peace.

i am air
propelling life into my lungs
pushing my heart to beat
constant until the last

i am a sign of the air
floating inspiration
breathing plumes and trails of shape
colour   texture
and rainbow bubbles of words
floating by
to the delight of children

i am the airy fairy
wings forever aloft with the breath
of too many ideas
like uncontained bubbles
caught in the whimsy of draughts
on a breezy day

i am air and traveller
the space above and below
both breath and heartbeat

i am air

www.ingramcontent.com/pod-product-compliance
Lightning Source LLC
Chambersburg PA
CBHW062148100526
44589CB00014B/1739